AF257948

Color & Read

Cover Design by humeraanwar10
Illustrations by humeraanwaar10

ISBN-13: 9781703638578
First Edition

For information about Color & Read parties, bulk or corporate purchases, please contact:

Kimberly M. Bailey
www.colorandread.com
www.facebook.com/colorandread
info@colorandread.com
901-877-4493

I, Sharon Pratt Dixon Kelly, became the first African American woman to serve as mayor of a major American city.

We are Barack and Michelle Obama, the first African American President and First Lady of the United States of America.

African American Firsts in Government

```
N  O  T  S  G  N  A  L  R  E  C  R  E  M  N  H  O  J
Y  D  K  T  M  J  C  J  P  U  T  P  U  N  P  X  Y  A
R  O  B  E  R  T  W  E  A  V  E  R  M  V  B  O  O  M
K  S  I  M  I  C  H  E  L  L  E  O  B  A  M  A  N  Y
R  I  N  U  A  R  B  Y  L  E  S  O  M  L  O  R  A  C
I  D  G  K  A  G  G  S  A  J  B  C  Y  D  Y  E  Y  S
E  V  O  L  U  A  E  D  R  U  O  B  A  Y  M  D  U  L
N  G  L  S  I  R  R  A  H  A  I  C  I  R  T  A  P  A
J  L  G  U  I  S  E  K  O  T  S  L  R  A  C  G  A  M
C  K  Q  Q  V  U  I  U  Y  L  A  N  C  I  C  X  P  A
T  G  E  M  D  R  O  X  Z  J  P  P  H  X  S  U  K  B
E  D  P  D  T  Z  A  S  J  L  K  S  J  F  S  A  V  O
Q  S  H  I  R  L  E  Y  C  H  I  S  H  O  L  M  E  K
T  K  G  T  X  Z  A  D  F  T  U  N  N  Y  R  U  N  C
X  A  N  G  B  G  A  S  T  T  M  N  S  J  F  C  T  A
A  W  T  N  Y  F  F  X  A  Z  K  R  U  Z  L  P  J  R
R  E  D  L  I  W  S  A  L  G  U  O  D  M  P  P  F  A
J  F  Z  Y  H  O  W  Y  G  V  O  Y  I  T  C  I  L  B
```

Barack Obama	Ludmya Bourdeau Love
Carl Stokes	Michelle Obama
Carol Mosely Braun	Patricia Harris
Douglas Wilder	Robert Weaver
John Mercer Langston	Shirley Chisholm

I am Theodore Sedgewick Wright. I became the first African American graduate from an American Theological school.

I am Ruth Simmons.
The first African
American to be
named President of
an Ivy League
university.

I, William Wells Brown, was the first African American to publish works in several major literary genres.

I am Hazel W. Johnson, the first African American woman to become a general in the U.S. Army.

I am James McCune Smith, the first African American to be awarded a degree in medicine.

I am Eugene James (Jacques) Bullard, the first African American combat aviator.

I, Mae Jemison, became the first African American woman in space in September of 1992.

I am Benjamin O. Davis Sr., the first African American to be named a general in the American military.

African American Firsts in Sports

```
B  T  O  T  N  O  S  N  H  O  J  K  C  A  J  H  Q  I
N  G  Q  E  G  R  Z  A  T  M  B  M  H  G  R  S  Y  C
Z  O  K  Z  R  O  L  Y  A  T  L  L  A  H  S  R  A  M
D  I  S  T  S  I  V  A  D  I  N  A  H  S  Y  E  X  F
L  M  M  N  S  K  Q  P  E  M  K  L  J  B  O  W  Q  R
A  K  T  D  I  R  K  L  I  P  K  V  Q  S  W  O  A  E
B  L  T  H  R  B  B  U  S  L  R  Y  X  N  I  L  S  W
U  G  I  Y  Z  A  O  V  O  R  Y  R  O  I  L  F  A  O
V  E  G  C  K  E  L  R  J  Q  Z  S  C  U  L  A  M  R
S  O  E  Y  E  D  K  L  E  Q  B  G  J  W  I  T  O  H
B  R  R  S  M  C  A  G  O  I  T  C  F  C  E  T  H  T
J  G  W  B  S  C  O  X  G  P  K  I  G  S  O  E  T  E
K  E  O  S  G  X  X  A  M  Q  Z  C  W  I  '  N  I  I
Z  P  O  Q  U  I  E  O  C  S  E  T  A  R  R  O  B  L
Y  O  D  U  B  H  D  M  F  H  U  U  I  J  E  V  E  L
C  A  S  T  T  B  B  P  J  F  M  Q  I  R  E  J  D  I
R  G  J  L  S  S  F  A  C  E  X  A  S  F  F  M  G  W
T  E  A  Z  E  P  X  D  P  N  M  Y  N  G  W  H  X  C
```

Alice Coachman	Marshall Taylor
Althea Gibson	Shani Davis
Debi Thomas	Tiger Woods
Fritz Pollard	Vonetta Flowers
George Poage	Willie O'Ree
Jackie Robinson	Willie Thrower
Jack Johnson	

I'm Carl B. Stokes, the first African American mayor of a major U.S. city.

I am Constance Baker Motley, the first African American woman to hold a Federal Judgeship.

You can be the first artist in your family.

Draw a picture of yourself.

I am David Jones Peck, the first black man to graduate from an American medical school.

I am the author of the first known work of African American literature (the poem "Bars Fight"), Lucy Terry Prince.

Other African American Firsts

Licensed Pilot: Bessie Coleman

Millionaire: Madame C. J. Walker

Billionaire: Robert Johnson, owner of Black Entertainment Television; Oprah Winfrey

On a postage stamp: Booker T. Washington in 1940

Miss America: Vanessa Williams, 1984, representing New York. When Williams resigned, Suzette Charles, the runner-up and an African American, assumed the title. She represented New Jersey.

Explorer, North Pole: Matthew A. Henson accompanied Robert E. Peary

Explorer, South Pole: George Gibbs accompanied Richard Byrd.

Flight around the world: Barrington Irving from Miami Gardens, Florida, flew a Columbia 400 plane named *Inspiration* around the world in 96 days, 150 hours.